EXPLORING COUNTRIES

Australia

HEATHER C. HUDAK

MEDIA ENHANCED BOOKS
AV2 BY WEIGL™
ADDED VALUE • AUDIO VISUAL

www.av2books.com

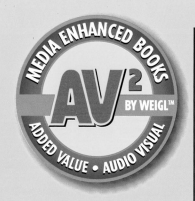

AV² provides enriched content that supplements and complements this book. Weigl's AV² books strive to create inspired learning and engage young minds in a total learning experience.

Your AV² Media Enhanced books come alive with...

Audio
Listen to sections of the book read aloud.

Key Words
Study vocabulary, and complete a matching word activity.

Video
Watch informative video clips.

Quizzes
Test your knowledge.

Embedded Weblinks
Gain additional information for research.

Slide Show
View images and captions, and prepare a presentation.

Try This!
Complete activities and hands-on experiments.

... and much, much more!

Go to **www.av2books.com**, and enter this book's unique code.

BOOK CODE

P 6 4 5 3 3 8

AV² by Weigl brings you media enhanced books that support active learning.

Published by AV² by Weigl
350 5th Avenue, 59th Floor
New York, NY 10118
Websites: www.av2books.com   www.weigl.com

Library of Congress Cataloging-in-Publication Data

Hudak, Heather C., 1975-
 Australia / Heather C. Hudak.
   pages cm. — (Exploring countries)
 Includes index.
 ISBN 978-1-4896-3054-4 (hard cover : alk. paper) — ISBN 978-1-4896-3055-1 (soft cover : alk. paper) — ISBN 978-1-4896-3056-8 (single user ebook) — ISBN 978-1-4896-3057-5 (multi-user ebook)
 1. Australia—Juvenile literature. 2. Australia—Description and travel—Juvenile literature. I. Title.
 DU96.H833 2014
 994—dc23   2014038995

Printed in the United States of America in Brainerd, Minnesota
1 2 3 4 5 6 7 8 9 19 18 17 16 15

012015
WEP160115

Project Coordinator Heather Kissock
Art Director Terry Paulhus

Contents

Australia Overview

Australia is the only country that occupies an entire continent. It is sometimes called the "land down under" because the country is located below the **equator**. Australia's diverse landscapes include rainforests, mountain ranges, and **plains**. Much of the country's interior is made up of deserts and dry grassland regions. This area is known as the outback. Australia is home to the Great Barrier Reef. Located off the northeast coast, it is the world's largest **coral** reef. Most of the country's people live in cities and other built-up areas along the southeast coast. Australia has a strong **economy**, and many of its people enjoy a high quality of life.

Sea turtles and colorful fish swim among the corals of the Great Barrier Reef.

Sydney Harbor Bridge is the largest steel arch bridge in the world and a popular tourist attraction.

Koalas live in eastern Australian forests and spend almost all their time in the trees.

Millions of sheep are raised for their wool, which is sheared, or cut off, once a year.

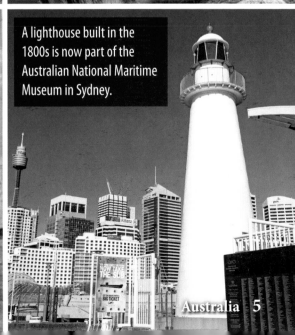

A lighthouse built in the 1800s is now part of the Australian National Maritime Museum in Sydney.

Exploring
Australia

With an area of about 2,966,150 square miles (7,682,300 square kilometers), Australia is the sixth-largest country in the world. It has a coastline of more than 20,000 miles (32,000 kilometers). The mainland stretches more than 2,500 miles (4,000 km) from west to east. It extends about 2,375 miles (3,825 km) from north to south. The country also includes the island of Tasmania, located south of the southeastern coast. Australia is divided into six states. They are New South Wales, Queensland, South Australia, Tasmania, Victoria, and Western Australia. The country also has two territories, the Australian Capital Territory (ACT) and Northern Territory.

Indian Ocean

AUST

Great Victoria Desert

Southern Ocean

N

Great Victoria
Desert

Map Legend

Australia

Land

Water

Lake Eyre

Great Victoria Desert

Tasmania

Capital City

SCALE

500 Miles

500 Kilometers

Great Victoria Desert

The Great Victoria Desert covers about 150,000 square miles (390,000 sq. km). It is the largest desert in Australia. Located in the southern part of the country, it is the sixth-largest desert in the world.

Lake Eyre

RALIA

Lake Eyre

Canberra

📍 **Canberra**

Tasmania

Tasmania

Lake Eyre

Lake Eyre is a saltwater lake in South Australia. The lake is often dry, since the area receives very little rain. It fills completely only about twice every 100 years. The lake has the lowest point on the continent, which is 50 feet (15 meters) below sea level.

Tasmania

Tasmania was connected to Australia until about 12,000 years ago. Then, ocean water levels rose, covering the land between the two regions. Tasmania has a total area of more than 26,000 square miles (67,000 sq. km). Much of the land is in national parks and other protected areas.

Canberra

Located in the ACT, Canberra is the capital of Australia. More than 350,000 people live in the city. The headquarters of Australia's national government, Canberra is also known for its universities and museums.

LAND AND CLIMATE

In northern Queensland, rainforests and waterfalls, such as Millaa Millaa Falls, are found in many coastal areas.

Much of Australia's land is plains and **plateaus**. The country is divided into three land regions. They are the Eastern Highlands, Central Lowlands, and Western Plateau.

The Eastern Highlands region includes high plateaus and mountain ranges, as well as low plains, sandy beaches, and rocky cliffs. Stretching from the northeastern Cape York **Peninsula** to Tasmania's south coast, the Eastern Highlands receive the most rainfall of Australia's three regions. The highest mountains are located in the southeast and are known as the Australian Alps.

Australia's Central Lowlands is a flat region that receives little rain. The Eastern Highlands block winds from the Pacific that carry moisture from reaching the country's interior. Many inland riverbeds remain dry, except during rare periods of heavy rainfall. A large supply of underground fresh water, known as the Great Artesian Basin, lies below the lowlands. Grass and shrubs cover much of the area, while other parts are sandy desert.

Much of the Western Plateau region is made up of flat land. Australia's four major deserts cover a large portion of this area. There are also low mountain ranges, as well as a number of individual mountains.

Australia's climate is mostly warm and dry. On the southwest coast, the city of Perth has cool, moist winters and warm, dry summers. The northern areas of Australia are in the **tropics**. In Queensland's tropical rainforests, an average of 159 inches (405 centimeters) of rain falls each year.

Australia's eastern and southern coasts receive about 40 to 60 inches (100 to 150 cm) of rain per year. Southern areas of the Eastern Highlands receive snow in winter. As in all countries of the Southern Hemisphere, winter months in Australia are the summer months in the northern half of Earth.

Land and Climate BY THE NUMBERS

7,310 Feet
Height of Mount Kosciusko in the Australian Alps, Australia's highest peak. (2,228 m)

ABOUT 33% Portion of Australia's land that is desert.

1,609 Miles Length of the Murray River, Australia's longest river. (2,589 km)

123° Fahrenheit
Highest temperature ever recorded in Australia, in Oodnadatta, South Australia, in 1960. (50.7° Celsius)

The Eastern Highlands are also known as the Great Dividing Range.

PLANTS AND ANIMALS

Many **species** of plants and animals in Australia cannot be found anywhere else on Earth. For millions of years, the island of Australia has been separated from other areas of land. Its plants and animals adapted in unique ways to conditions in Australia.

Nearly 1,000 types of acacias grow in Australia. These strong shrubs and trees with bright flowers are found in nearly every region of the continent. Another common plant is the **eucalyptus**, or gum tree. Its flowers may be white, yellow, pink, or red. In dry areas, some of Australia's flowering plants may not bloom for years. Flowers appear only after a heavy rainfall.

Many of Australia's best-known animals are **marsupials**. The country has more than 140 kinds of marsupials. They include kangaroos, koalas, wallabies, and wombats. **Mammals** that lay eggs, such as the platypus, also live in Australia. Platypuses hunt for food under water, and their webbed feet help make them good swimmers.

There are about 750 bird species in Australia. They include the emu, kookaburra, and lyrebird. The emu, which cannot fly, is Australia's largest bird.

1988
Year that the golden wattle, a type of acacia, was named the official floral emblem of Australia.

300 Feet

Height that the southern eucalyptus tree can reach, making it the world's tallest flowering plant. (90 m)

19 MILLION
Number of kangaroos living in Australia.

Large kangaroos use their tails for balancing. Some kangaroos can weigh as much as 200 pounds (90 kilograms).

NATURAL RESOURCES

Australia has many natural resources. About two-thirds of the country's land is suitable for farming or ranching. Of this land, 90 percent is used for grazing animals.

Some ranchers raise beef cattle for meat. Australia has many sheep farms, and it is the world's largest seller of wool to other nations. Wheat, sugarcane, and grapes are some of the crops that grow well in Australia's climate.

Australia's minerals include copper, gold, lead, iron ore, and uranium. The country is the world's leading bauxite producer. Bauxite is used in making aluminum. Australia is also a world leader in coal production. It mines more than 95 percent of the world's opals. These gemstones are used in jewelry. Diamonds are also mined in Australia.

Natural Resources BY THE NUMBERS

728 Million Pounds
Amount of wool that is produced in Australia yearly. (330 million kg)

28.5 Million
Number of cattle in Australia.

79%
Portion of the country's electricity that comes from burning coal and other **fossil fuels**.

The Kalgoorlie Super Pit gold mine in Western Australia is one of the world's largest open-cut mines. In this type of mine, the surface of the land is removed to reach the ore.

TOURISM

Tourism is a major industry in Australia. Each year, more than 6 million people from all parts of the world visit the country. About 20 percent of visitors are from New Zealand. People from China, the United Kingdom, and the United States also visit in large numbers.

Australia offers a wide range of attractions. In Sydney, Australia's largest city, people can tour the Sydney Opera House or The Rocks, Sydney's historic area. The Rocks is where Australia's first European settlement began.

Cadman's Cottage in The Rocks area of Sydney is the oldest building in Australia. It dates back to 1816.

In Melbourne, Australia's second-largest city, tourists can shop in the Block Arcade. This large indoor shopping area is located in the city's historic business district. Many people visit Federation Square to enjoy its restaurants, art exhibits, and indoor or outdoor music and theater performances.

Melbourne's Federation Square is home to museums such as the National Gallery of Victoria.

Adventure-seekers can take a tour through the rugged outback in four-wheel-drive vehicles. Some choose to hike in Tasmania's remote areas. The island has one of the world's last remaining temperate rainforests, which are rainforests not located in tropical regions.

Many tourists visit Uluru, a sacred place to Australia's Aborigines, or indigenous people. Located in central Australia, Uluru is one of the largest **monoliths** in the world. Also known as Ayers Rock, Uluru can be viewed on a walking, camel, helicopter, or motorcycle tour. Aboriginal Australians prefer that visitors not climb Uluru.

The Great Barrier Reef is one of the most diverse plant and animal **ecosystems** in the world. It contains more than 1,500 miles (2,500 km) of coral reef. Visitors can sail around the reef, dive through its clear depths, or snorkel in the water. Many tourists visit the beaches on the mainland, in Tasmania, or on Kangaroo Island. This resort area is located off the coast near the city of Adelaide in South Australia.

Uluru is made of a kind of sandstone that appears to change color depending on the Sun's position in the sky.

More Than 1,500
Number of fish species living in the Great Barrier Reef.

1,140 feet Height of Uluru. (350 m)

2,679 Number of guests who can be seated in the Sydney Opera House's Concert Hall.

7 Number of theme parks in Gold Coast, a resort city in southern Queensland. (40 km)

INDUSTRY

Australia is considered a **developed country**. Its yearly gross domestic product (GDP), the total value of goods and services the country produces, is almost $1 trillion. That gives Australia the 18th largest economy in the world.

Per capita GDP is a country's total GDP divided by the number of people who live there. Australia has a per capita GDP of $43,000. This figure is higher than in most other countries. It is similar to per capita GDP in Canada and many European countries with strong economies.

Manufacturing is important to the Australian economy. Products that are made in Australia include machinery, transportation equipment, chemicals, and steel. Many factories make food products using farm crops or meat from the country's livestock herds.

| Many Australians are well educated, which prepares them for high-tech jobs related to manufacturing.

Almost 12.5 million
Number of workers in Australia.

21 % Portion of Australian workers employed in the manufacturing and mining industries.

More Than $26 Billion
Value of the steel produced in Australia each year.

GOODS AND SERVICES

S ervice industries make up the largest part of Australia's economy. In service industries, workers provide a service to other people rather than produce goods. These workers include bankers, teachers, doctors and nurses, people employed in stores and restaurants, tour guides, and other workers who help tourists.

Trade with other countries is important to Australia's economy. The amount of trade has increased greatly in recent years. Major products that Australia **exports** include coal, iron ore, gold, meat, and wool. Major **imports** are machinery, computers, and office equipment.

Much of Australia's trade is with nations in Asia. The country sells more goods to China and buys more from China than it does from any other nation. After China, the United States is the next-largest source of products imported by Australia.

Goods and Services BY THE NUMBERS

About 75%
Portion of Australian workers employed in service industries.

62%
Percentage of Australia's exports that go to the Asian countries of China, Japan, South Korea, and India.

More Than $250 Billion
Value of Australia's exports each year.

Long trains carry iron ore to Australia's ports for shipment to other countries.

INDIGENOUS PEOPLES

Many scientists believe the first Aborigines to reach Australia traveled there by boat from Southeast Asia about 50,000 years ago. Over time, many different groups developed in the various regions of the continent. Traditionally, Aboriginal Australians hunted animals and gathered plants for food. Often, groups moved from one place to another in different seasons to find the best food sources.

Traditional Aboriginal culture includes belief in the Dreaming, or Dreamtime. During the Dreaming, which began long ago and has no end, mythical beings created the natural world and all living things. They also created rules for how people should act and behave toward one another. Places where mythical beings performed important actions or were changed into natural objects became sacred sites.

When European settlers began arriving in the late 1700s, many Aborigines died in conflicts with the Europeans. Still more died from diseases brought to Australia for the first time by the settlers. Other Aborigines were pushed off their traditional lands. Many were forced onto **reserves**. In 2008, Australia's government apologized for the treatment of Aborigines in the past.

About 750,000
Number of Aborigines who were living in Australia when European settlers arrived.

50% Portion of Aborigines in what is now the Sydney area who died of smallpox within one year of the arrival of European settlers.

Year that all Aborigines gained Australian citizenship.

Australia is home to some of the world's oldest rock art, or paintings on rock. In some areas, Aboriginal rock art dates back 40,000 years or more.

THE AGE OF EXPLORATION

In the 1500s, explorers from several European countries searched for a large landmass in the Southern Hemisphere. Spanish and Portuguese ships had reached New Guinea by 1526. In 1606, Spaniard Luis Vaez de Torres sailed around the southern coast of New Guinea, showing that it was an island, not part of a continent. The body of water de Torres sailed through, which separates New Guinea and Australia, is now named the Torres Strait. Also in 1606, Dutch explorer Willem Jansz became the first European to land on the Australian continent.

Dutch explorer Abel Tasman sailed around parts of Australia in 1642. Tasman visited a nearby landmass, which he named Van Diemen's Land in honor of a Dutch official. In 1856, the land was renamed Tasmania.

By the late 1600s, British ships were exploring the southern Pacific region. British sea captain James Cook sailed along the eastern coast of Australia in 1770 and claimed the area for Great Britain. He named the region New South Wales.

The Age of Exploration by the NUMBERS

80 Miles Distance between New Guinea and Australia across the Torres Strait. (130 km)

1802–1803 Years when British explorer Matthew Flinders sailed around Australia.

1814 Year that Flinders published a map of the Australian coastline.

Captain Cook gave the name Botany Bay to the waters near present-day Sydney because of the great variety of plants in the area.

EARLY SETTLERS

In 1788, British Captain Arthur Phillip built the first permanent European settlement in Australia. Phillip set sail from Portsmouth, Great Britain, on May 13, 1787, with 11 ships called the First Fleet. More than 1,400 people were on these ships, and nearly half of them were convicts taken from British prisons. The fleet arrived in Botany Bay on January 18, 1788. A few days later, on January 26, the ships sailed to Port Jackson, where the settlers built a **colony**. This settlement grew into the city of Sydney.

A certificate of freedom released a convict after seven years of labor in a penal colony.

The practice of shipping prisoners overseas was called transportation. Few of the prisoners sent to Australia had experience farming or building houses. The lack of farming skills and the poor soil at the site of the settlement made it difficult for the Port Jackson colony to succeed. In the early years, there were severe food shortages. British prisoners were transported to establish settlements, known as penal colonies, in other parts of Australia. By the 1790s, settlers who were not prisoners began arriving, too.

By the early 1800s, a wall to protect the colony had been built around Port Jackson.

The capital cities of Australia's states are built at the locations of early settlements in those areas. Hobart, Tasmania, was first settled in 1804. In 1824, a penal colony was established along the Brisbane River. This settlement became the city of Brisbane, the capital of Queensland. Captain James Stirling led a group of free settlers to build a colony along the Swan River in 1829. Located in Western Australia, this settlement became known as Perth. A settlement at Port Phillip Bay was established in 1835. Today, Port Phillip is known as Melbourne. Adelaide, in South Australia, was settled in 1836.

By 1839, there were twice as many free settlers as there were convicts in Australia. The British government officially ended the policy of transporting prisoners there in 1868. Six separate British colonies developed on the continent during the 1800s. In 1901, the colonies united to form the independent country of Australia.

Australians celebrate their national holiday, called Australia Day, on January 26 each year. However, many Aboriginal Australians do not celebrate the holiday. Some call the date Invasion Day.

Port Arthur in Tasmania was a penal colony between 1830 and 1877. The building where many convicts lived is now a historic site that can be visited.

Early Settlers BY THE NUMBERS

8 Months, 5 Days
Length of the First Fleet's voyage.

18% Portion of the prisoners transported to Australia who were female.

ABOUT 160,000
Total number of British convicts transported to Australia.

POPULATION

Australia's population has grown a great deal since the first British colony began. Today, more than 23 million people live in the country. However, Australia's **population density** is lower than in most other nations. On average, there are fewer than eight people per square mile (three per sq. km) of land.

The population is not spread out evenly. Few people live in **rural** areas. About nine out of ten Australians live in cities or towns. New South Wales is the state with the largest population. About 7.5 million people live there.

Most Australians are of European **ancestry**. Aborigines make up less than 1 percent of the population. Until the late 1940s, most of Australia's **immigrants** came from Great Britain or Ireland. After the end of World War II in 1945, the Australian government encouraged Europeans who were homeless due to the fighting to move to the country. As a result, many immigrants came to Australia from Greece, Italy, Yugoslavia, Germany, and the Netherlands. Since the 1970s, a large number of immigrants have come to Australia from Southeast Asia, India, and other parts of Asia.

7% Percentage of Australians who have Asian ancestry.

About 25%
Portion of Australia's population born in a different country.

82 Number of years, on average, that people born in Australia today can expect to live, longer than in almost all other countries.

The population of Darwin, capital city of the Northern Territory, is more than 129,000. The Northern Territory is one of the fastest-growing regions of Australia.

POLITICS AND GOVERNMENT

Australia's government is based on the British system. Officially, Australia is a **constitutional monarchy**. The British queen or king is the head of state.

Australia has a written **constitution**, which went into effect in 1901. The constitution divides the government into three parts. The Parliament, or legislature, makes laws. The executive branch puts the laws into practice. The **judicial branch** upholds the laws.

Parliament has two houses, or parts, called the Senate and House of Representatives. Their members are elected by the voters. After an election, the political party that wins the most seats in the House of Representatives controls the government. The leader of this party is the head of the government and is called the prime minister. He or she selects members of Parliament to manage specific government departments, such as education, agriculture, or defense. These people are called government ministers.

Each state or territory has its own government. It is responsible for local matters. The heads of state governments are called premiers.

2010
Year in which Julia Gillard became the first female prime minister of Australia.

150 Number of members in the House of Representatives.

76 Number of members in the Senate.

Parliament House in Canberra, where the Senate and House of Representatives meet, first opened in 1988.

CULTURAL GROUPS

Many different cultural groups make up Australia's population. Since 1945, more than 7 million people have moved to Australia from all parts of the world. Canberra celebrates its cultural communities during the three-day Multicultural Festival. This annual city-wide celebration features food, entertainment, and crafts from many cultures. These include Polish, Indonesian, Tibetan, Scottish, and Greek.

Aboriginal Australians live in all parts of the country. A majority are in New South Wales or Queensland.

In Sydney, many people of Asian descent live in the area known as Cabramatta. Australia's largest Asian festival, the Lunar New Year celebration, takes place in Cabramatta. There are fireworks displays, cooking demonstrations, martial arts performances, and parades. In Freedom Plaza, shops and restaurants sell Asian products and foods. Large Buddhist temples are located nearby. Thousands of people, both Asian and non-Asian, gather in Cabramatta to celebrate the Lunar New Year.

Chinese people often perform the Lion Dance as part of the Lunar New Year celebration. The Lion Dance is thought to bring joy, fortune, and good luck.

English is the language most commonly spoken in Australia. Australians use many slang terms in their speech. For example, anything excellent is a "bottler." Something of poor quality is "bodgy." Other than English, commonly spoken languages include Italian, Greek, Vietnamese, Chinese, and Aboriginal languages.

Many aspects of the Aborigines' traditional culture have been lost. However, a number of Aborigines are working to preserve their culture. This includes their native languages.

About 60 percent of Australians are Christians. The largest number of Christians follow a Protestant faith, and about one-fourth of Australians are Roman Catholic. Other religions practiced by Australians include Buddhism, Hinduism, and Islam, the faith of Muslims.

The types of food popular in Australia have been influenced by British cooking. However, traditional foods from many other cultures are also enjoyed by millions of Australians. Cooking outdoors on a barbeque is common in Australia. Since the country is surrounded by ocean waters, seafood is part of many meals. The spicy vegetable spread Vegemite is a lunch or snack food.

St. Mary's Cathedral, the largest Catholic church in Sydney, was built in the 1800s.

ARTS AND ENTERTAINMENT

The national government supports the arts and entertainment in Australia. It provides funds for cultural exhibitions, as well as film and television productions. Symphony orchestras, opera companies, and theater groups also receive support. Government **grants** for writers, painters, musicians, and composers help these people create new works.

Opera Australia is one of the country's leading performing arts companies. It has its regular season at the Sydney Opera House and Arts Center Melbourne. The opera company also has performed at Sydney Harbor and the Gold Coast beach, as well as in towns across the country.

A sculpture by the artist Henry Moore stands outside the National Gallery of Australia in Canberra.

Opera Australia performs many different works. They include Giacomo Puccini's opera *Manon Lescaut*, about a young woman in 18th-century France.

Australia has many museums. Canberra's National Gallery of Australia has more than 160,000 artworks. The National Gallery of Victoria is known for its collection of Australian Aboriginal art. At the Museum of Old and New Art in Hobart, Tasmania, visitors are given a handheld electronic device. It determines which exhibit the visitor is viewing and provides information about that piece of art.

Some of the world's best-known film actors come from Australia. Although she was born in Hawai'i, Nicole Kidman moved to Sydney with her family when she was a young child. Before making her Hollywood debut in the 1989 movie *Dead Calm*, Kidman starred in many Australian film and television productions. Actor Naomi Watts was born in Great Britain but moved to Australia as a teenager. Hugh Jackman, well known for his role as Wolverine/Logan in the X-Men movies, is from Sydney.

Australia is also home to many talented authors. In 1973, fiction writer Patrick White won the Nobel Prize in Literature. He was the first Australian to win this award. His books include *The Tree of Man*, *Voss*, and *Riders in the Chariot*. In 1964, poet Oodgeroo Noonuccal was the first Aboriginal Australian to publish a book of poetry. It is titled *We Are Going*.

The Australian Ballet stages more than 200 dance performances each year, including the 19th-century ballet *Don Quixote*.

SPORTS

Australia's warm climate gives people many chances to enjoy outdoor sports and recreation activities. From team games to golf, a wide range of sports are popular in Australia. Most large communities have professional and amateur sports teams.

Cricket is one of Australia's most popular sports. The game is played on an oval field by two teams of 11 players. Players use a bat that is round on one side and flat on the other to hit a ball a little larger than a baseball. Matches can take several days to play. The Australian national team competes against teams from around the world, including Great Britain, India, and the West Indies.

Michael Clarke began playing for Australia's national cricket team in 2004.

Australian rules football, rugby, and soccer, which is called football in Australia, are three major field sports. Each team has between 11 and 18 players, depending on the sport. Teams try to score points by pushing past the opposing team toward a goal on the other end of the playing field. In Australia, these sports involve a great deal of contact between players, who wear little or no padding to protect them from injury.

Australian rules football is Australia's most popular spectator sport.

Netball is another popular Australian sport. It is often played by women. Like basketball, netball is played on a court. Instead of baskets, there is a goal with a hoop at each end of the court. Players pass the ball up the court.

Many Australians enjoy water sports, such as swimming, surfing, rowing, and diving. Hiking and camping, called bushwalking in Australia, is also popular. Many Australians play tennis, and the country's professional players have won a number of major international championships.

Cathy Freeman is one of Australia's most successful track and field athletes. In 1990, at the age of 16, she became the first Aboriginal Australian runner to win a gold medal at the **Commonwealth Games**. Freeman made history again in 1992, when she became the first Aboriginal track-and-field athlete to represent Australia in the Olympic Games. Four years later, she took home the silver medal in the 400-meter event at the 1996 Olympics in Atlanta, Georgia.

At the 2000 Olympics, held in Sydney, Cathy Freeman won the gold medal in the 400-meter race.

Mapping Australia

We use many tools to interpret maps and to understand the locations of features such as cities, states, lakes, and rivers. The map below has many tools to help interpret information on the map of Australia.

Map of Australia

Indian Ocean

Torres Strait

Cape York Peninsula

Darwin

Gulf of Carpenteria

Great Barrier Reef

Pacific Ocean

Northern Territory

Queensland

Alice Springs

▲ Uluru

Western Australia

South Australia

Lake Eyre

Great Victoria Desert

• Brisbane
Gold Coast

New South Wales

Perth

Murray River

Canberra

• Sydney

Adelaide

Australian Capital Territory

Kangaroo Island

Victoria

• Melbourne

Southern Ocean

Tasmania
• Hobart

MAP LEGEND

★ Capital City   ⌄ River   ╲ Longitude & Latitude

● City   ·—·— State Border   ▢ Australia

〰 Body of Water   ▲ Uluru   ▢ Other Countries

N W E S

SCALE

0   400 Miles

0   400 Kilometers

Mapping Tools

- The compass rose shows north, south, east, and west. The points in between represent northeast, northwest, southeast, and southwest.

- The map scale shows that the distances on a map represent much longer distances in real life. If you measure the distance between objects on a map, you can use the map scale to calculate the actual distance in miles or kilometers between those two points.

- The lines of latitude and longitude are long lines that appear on maps. The lines of latitude run east to west and measure how far north or south of the equator a place is located. The lines of longitude run north to south and measure how far east or west of the Prime Meridian a place is located. A location on a map can be found by using the two numbers where latitude and longitude meet. This number is called a coordinate and is written using degrees and direction. For example, the city of Adelaide would be found at 35°S and 139°E on a map.

Map It!

Using the map and the appropriate tools, complete the activities below.

Locating with latitude and longitude

1. Which Australian state is found at 30°S and 125°E?
2. What body of water is found at 15°S and 140°E?
3. What place is found on the map using the coordinates 38°S and 145°E?

Distances between points

4. Using the map scale and a ruler, calculate the approximate distance between the cities of Perth and Sydney.
5. Calculate the approximate distance between Brisbane and Hobart.
6. Using the map scale to figure out the answer, what landmark is found about 290 miles (470 km) from Alice Springs?

ANSWERS 1. Western Australia 2. Gulf of Carpentaria 3. Melbourne 4. 2,000 miles (3,300 km) 5. 1,100 miles (1,800 km) 6. Uluru

Quiz Time

Test your knowledge of Australia by answering these questions.

1 Which city is located where the first European settlement in Australia was established?

2 What portion of the world's opals are mined in three Australian states?

3 Which country's citizens make up about 20 percent of visitors to Australia?

4 Where is the lowest geographic point in Australia?

5 When did Aborigines first reach Australia?

6 What is the name often used for Australia's dry, rugged interior regions?

7 How many times has Australia won the International Cricket Council's World Cup?

8 What is the capital of Australia?

9 Australia's government is modeled after what country's system?

10 How many kangaroos live in Australia?

ANSWERS

1. Sydney
2. 95 percent
3. New Zealand
4. In Lake Eyre
5. About 50,000 years ago
6. The outback
7. Four
8. Canberra
9. Great Britain's
10. About 19 million

Key Words

ancestry: people who lived in the past from whom a culture or person has descended

colony: an area or country that is under the control of another country

Commonwealth Games: events in which athletes from countries that are members of the Commonwealth of Nations compete in various sports

constitution: a written document stating a country's basic principles and laws

constitutional monarchy: a system of government in which the powers of a hereditary ruler are limited by a country's constitution and laws

coral: the hard skeletons of tiny sea animals called corals that live in tropical ocean waters

developed country: a country that has many industries and relatively few poor people

economy: the wealth and resources of a country or area

ecosystems: communities of living things and resources

equator: an imaginary circle around Earth's surface that separates the Northern and Southern Hemispheres, or halves, of the planet

eucalyptus: a tall evergreen tree with a strong-smelling oil in its leaves

exports: sells goods to other countries

fossil fuels: fuels such as coal, natural gas, and oil that formed from the remains of plants and animals that lived long ago

grants: gifts of money, often to support a specific activity or project

immigrants: people who move to a new country or area to live

imports: goods that are bought from other countries

judicial branch: the part of a government that includes its courts

mammals: animals that have hair or fur and that feed mother's milk to their young

marsupials: animals that give birth to live young that the mother then carries in a pouch on her stomach

monoliths: very large blocks of stone

peninsula: an area of land surrounded on three sides by water

plains: flat, treeless areas

plateaus: flat areas of land raised above the surrounding area

population density: the number of people living in a certain area of land

reserves: areas of land set aside for Aborigines

rural: relating to the countryside

species: groups of individuals with common characteristics

tropics: the area of Earth closest to the equator, where the weather is warm year-round

Index

Log on to www.av2books.com

AV² by Weigl brings you media enhanced books that support active learning. Go to www.av2books.com, and enter the special code found on page 2 of this book. You will gain access to enriched and enhanced content that supplements and complements this book. Content includes video, audio, weblinks, quizzes, a slide show, and activities.

AV² Online Navigation

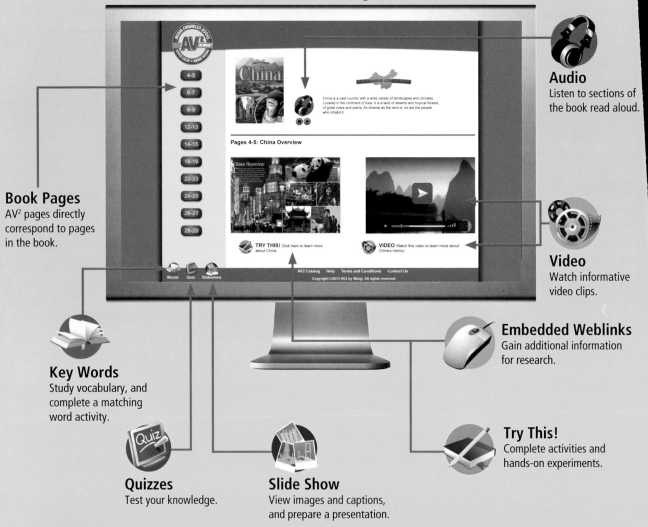

Book Pages
AV² pages directly correspond to pages in the book.

Audio
Listen to sections of the book read aloud.

Video
Watch informative video clips.

Key Words
Study vocabulary, and complete a matching word activity.

Embedded Weblinks
Gain additional information for research.

Quizzes
Test your knowledge.

Slide Show
View images and captions, and prepare a presentation.

Try This!
Complete activities and hands-on experiments.

AV² was built to bridge the gap between print and digital. We encourage you to tell us what you like and what you want to see in the future.

Sign up to be an AV² Ambassador at www.av2books.com/ambassador.

Due to the dynamic nature of the Internet, some of the URLs and activities provided as part of AV² by Weigl may have changed or ceased to exist. AV² by Weigl accepts no responsibility for any such changes. All media enhanced books are regularly monitored to update addresses and sites in a timely manner. Contact AV² by Weigl at 1-866-649-3445 or av2books@weigl.com with any questions, comments, or feedback.